The Great

I Am

Father, Son, Holy Spirit

by

Shayn Wallace Roby

Copyright ©2016 Shayn Wallace Roby

All Rights Reserved

ISBN-10: 978-1534917293

ISBN-13: 1534917292

Dedication

This book is dedicated to numerous people who helped me in my journey to come back to Christ after years of backsliding, and to those who helped foster a continued desire to continue in the ministry of Jesus Christ and in the fight for the soul of our nation.

My wife and best friend

Heather Nolan Roby

My parents and grandmother

Warner Scott Roby, Lela Wallace Roby, and Frances Wallace

My pastors

Ellis Clark, Bob Herndon, Keith Andrews,

and Wiley Drake

My fellow patriots and brothers in the Lord

Joe Messina The Real Side

Danny Peppers at The Stewart County Standard

My brothers and sisters in Zambia, Africa

Jack and Amber Mututwa

The House of Jeremiah, Long Beach, CA

Pastor Mark Maciel and Ed Ingram

Contents

Acknowledgements   pg5

Light: The Origin of All Matter   pg 6

Man's Place in God's Universe   pg 36

A God of Miracles   pg 76

A Word from the Author   pg 93

Acknowledgments

Thanks to my wife Heather for constantly encouraging me and sometimes reading the original drafts of this book, line by line, paragraph by paragraph.

Thanks to Kaylynn Smith Wilson for a wealth of material that helped frame my thinking.

Thanks to Glenn Beck for inspiring me to follow the breadcrumbs that God has laid down for me during the course of the most recent days of my life.

Thanks to Reverend James Robison, Dana Loesch, Ted Cruz, Pastor Tony Evans, Dr. Samuel Rodriguez, Reverend C.L. Bryant, and many other speakers at Restoring Freedom, Under God Indivisible, and Restoring Love in the summer of 2012 that helped frame my determination to become a part of the citizen media, and to inform our communities, states, nation, and world as The Original Light, The Great I Am directs me to do it.

Chapter 1

Light: The Origin of All Matter

One of the most frequently asked questions when exploring the mysteries surrounding the origins of the universe revolves around causation[1]. It's only natural for human beings to employ their finite minds around a starting point. The human mind wants to be able to point to a certain spot on the timeline of history, and say, "*This is where it all began.* " Perhaps a logical place to start for inquiring minds would be to start investigating where *matter* came from.

Even though non-believers in the Great I Am, the *Original Light* generally lack the intellectual honesty to admit it, scientific sources of so-called Ivy league quality eventually arrive at the question, "Where did the matter in the universe come from?"[2] As physicists struggle to explain the existence of exponentially greater amounts of matter than anti-matter (which in effect invalidates the hypothesis of a spherically symmetrical Big Bang)[3]left over from collisions between electrons and positrons, and protons and antiprotons[4]: Almost all reasonable scientific solutions to the question regarding the origin of matter eventually respond in kind with an origin that relates to light, and involve the equation made famous by Albert Einstein, $E=Mc^2$.   In summary of what Cornell graduate, and physics graduate student at Harvard University Sara Slater wrote at Ask an Astronomer[2] that "there was light in the beginning" and that light eventually decays into protons in response to the question, *"Where did the matter in the universe come from?"*, the question still remains to be answered after that, *"Where did light come from?"*.

Interestingly enough, as world renowned quantum physicist Michio Kaku has determined that "in all probability there is an unseen force that governs everything"[5], some experts from respected halls of academia have reached the conclusion that the origin of matter is indeed light. Curiously enough, the Holy Bible refers to Jehovah, the Father and Yeshua, the Lamb as the *Light of the universe*. Jehovah, or Yahweh, the Great I Am is all-knowing and omniscient. He (The Original Light) created the sun (secondary light) that emits electromagnetic radiation that can reach the Earth in approximately eight minutes. In one second, visible light and other forms of electromagnetic radiation, can circumnavigate planet Earth approximately seven times.[6]

Visible light is composed of a spectrum of colors that consists of red, orange, yellow, blue, indigo, and violet. Perhaps it is no coincidence that *the Original Light* used the spectrum of visible light to make His covenant with Noah in the form of a rainbow. This covenant made by the Great I Am, *the Original Light* with mankind established His promise that planet Earth in its entirety, would never again be almost destroyed at God's hand by flood waters. Unfortunately, those who would seek to defy His Holy Word have made a mockery of that covenant symbol by adopting the rainbow as a recognized label for the **lesbian, gay, bisexual**[7], and **trans-gendered**[8] movement.

Now, back to the question, "*Where did light come from?*" The Book of the Gospel of John in the Holy Bible says that light came from the *"true Light, which gives light to everyone, was coming into the world."*[9] It also says that "He was in the world, and the world was made through Him, and the world did not know Him."[10] In the beginning, He was the Word. He was with God and He was God.[11] Though he created the sun and moon to provide light for planet Earth, He did not need to do so for the sake of light, because there is unfathomable, brilliant luminosity around His countenance because of His glory.[12] Scripture describes the Original Light in the 21st chapter of the book of Revelation in reference to the New Jerusalem. Verse 23 refers to the brightness surrounding the very presence of our Lord:

verse 23 ***The city had no need of the sun or of the moon to shine in it, for the glory of God illuminated it***.[13] The book of First John in The Holy Bible says that "God is light, in Him is no darkness at all."[14] God's Holy Word states that our Lord is literally light itself, and at the same time is pure light in a metaphorical sense, because He is without sin. Jehovah abhors sin to the point that when Jesus, the Lamb took the sins of mankind upon Himself, He was unable to bear to look upon His Son, who at that particular moment was the sacrifice to pay the price for sin. He looked away as our Savior cried out in Aramaic, *"Eli, eli, lama sabachthani?"*, which translated into English is, *"My God why have you forsaken me?"*[15] In this brief moment when God looked away, for the first time, Jesus felt what it was like to experience a lack of intimacy with His Heavenly Father that He had always felt in fellowship with Jehovah. Soon thereafter, Jesus gave up the ghost. The moment that He died, the veil of the temple in

Jerusalem was ripped in half. The veil "separated the Holy of Holies—the earthly dwelling place of God's presence—from the rest of the temple where men dwelt. This signified that man was separated from God by sin."[16] Jesus Himself became the temple for all of humanity, the intercessor between Jehovah and mankind. At that point, the Old Covenant between man and God was replaced as The Lamb acted as the lamp that lights the path for all of humanity who are willing to follow Him , so that they might be able to be in the presence of the *Original Light.*[17]

Denial of the Deity of the Lamb, and of the sovereignty of the Great I Am has been taking place throughout history, since the fall of Adam and Eve in the garden. Modern day, worldly political pundits belittle

Christian morals and those who follow the Light on almost every network newscast, as they push the United States and other unGodly nations on toward the fate of judgement such as that endured by Israel and Judah when they played the harlot hundreds of years before the birth of Christ. Instead of following the Original Light, these talking heads follow the directive of the Counterfeit Light, or of his fallen angel minions (demons) who pose as deities. The name, *Lucifer*[18] comes from the Latin meaning "bringing light". Lucifer, Satan, Beelzebub, or Iblis (according to the Q'uaran) was the first being who dared to try to put himself ahead of God in his heart.

According to **Isaiah 14: 13 and 14**[19], in The Holy Bible Lucifer said,

> 13 ....m'I will ascend into heaven,
> nI will exalt my throne above the stars of God;
> I will also sit on the ᵒmount of the congregation
> ᵖOn the farthest sides of the north;

[14]   I will ascend above the heights of the clouds,
¶I will be like the Most High.'

He (Satan) manipulated a third of the angels in heaven into doing the same thing, was cast down out of heaven[20]. At this point, some believe that God destroyed the Earth, leaving it void and without form [21], before he created the plants animals and mankind.

After the creation of the Garden of Eden, Lucifer lied to Eve, then to Adam, and the counterfeit light has been lying ever since and has been attempting to seduce mankind into placing worldly desires and pleasures of the flesh ahead of the Righteousness of The Almighty. And even though the intellectually gifted Albert Einstein did not believe so[22], God gave man the ability to choose the path of the Original Light, or to forge his own path through the mazes of the deceitful one.

The deceitful one, or the counterfeit light is often known as Satan, Old Scratch, or the Devil. He is an established fixture with a semi-official place in the Democratic Party in the United States as their primary guide for community organizing, as *Rules for Radicals* (the political playbook for liberals) by Saul Alinksy is dedicated to the Counterfeit Light on the inside of its front cover by Alinsky himself.[23] He has guided this American political party toward being sympathetic to the false religions of secular humanism (subtle, but a religion nonetheless) and Islam , of which its so-called holy book, the Q'uaran agrees with the charge made by Iblis (Satan) that God is a deceiver.[24] The Holy Bible makes it clear that God's Word is Truth. The book of Isaiah in Chapter forty and verse eight says that *"the grass withers, and the flowers fall, but the Word of our God endures forever."*[25]

These radicals (liberals) have managed to keep the worship of and teaching about Jesus out of American public schools, even though it is clear that the intent of our founding fathers was to have *paid teachers* within our public schools teaching about the Gospel of Jesus[26].

He (Satan) has infiltrated the American Republican Party as well, as the Karl Rove wing of the GOP secretly embraces the baby butchers at Planned Parenthood[27]. Though many statists and scientists with mindsets akin to atheistic denial would challenge the existence of The Original Light as an omniscient all-powerful spiritual entity[28], Jesus has told us that He is the Alpha and the Omega, the beginning and the end, and that one day every knee shall bow and acknowledge that He is Lord.[29] Of course, God's Holy Word speaks of wars and rumors of wars that will take place before that day of judgement. Those nations that fall under the hand of tyranny as a result of the faithlessness of the wicked and Godless majority still can count on His promise of being restored through trusting in the *Original Light*, The Great I Am, but only when *repentance* has taken place. **In the 2nd Book of Chronicles,**[30] Jehovah promised King Solomon that if His people, who are called by His (God's) name will humble themselves, and pray, and seek His face, and turn from their wicked ways, then He will hear them from heaven, and will forgive their sin, and heal their land. [30]

The flip side of this covenant though is that every time God's people turn from Him, they can expect to be plucked out by the roots and delivered into captivity. This occurred to Israel and Judah as they were taken into captivity by the Assyrians, Babylonians, and Medes and Persians after having worshipped other gods and choosing not to serve the Almighty. God heard the sincere prayers of the oppressed though and allowed them to be restored to a position of safety as they sought His righteousness as when the Original Light shined on Esther and made her Queen in the Court of Persian King Ahasuerus (Xerxes),[31] and won so much favor in his sight that the Hebrew people were brought from a position of oppression and danger into a position of favor and prosperity.

Why does humanity repeatedly deny the Supreme Power of the *Original Light*, the Great I Am? Throughout scripture in The Holy Bible, God's chosen people fell away from Him and worshipped counterfeit or substitute gods. Only after they (the Israelites) were drawn into hardship would a remnant recognize that their circumstances were indeed a consequence of their lack of faithfulness. A modern day false god that rests in the hearts and minds of many non-Christians is the exaltation of science and Mother Earth. One argument that these modernday skeptics of an origin that corresponds with the Bible's account of causation cling to stems from scientific academia reigning from the disciplines of geology, physics and chemistry. These "masterminds" from the almighty community of academia insist that they can determine the age of matter through radiometric dating. According to the **United States Geological Survey, current estimates of the age of our planet** are projected at 4.4 to 4.6 billion years old.[32] Curiously enough, the USGS concedes in the very same article that gave this estimate that "samples for dating are carefully selected to avoid those that are altered, contaminated, or disturbed by later heating or chemical events". [33] The reason for such a disclaimer being needed is quite apparent. Radiometric dating must assume constant temperature and pressure in order to be considered accurate and valid, neither of which a single scientist can guarantee to have occurred over a period of even a *few hundred* years, much less a *few billion*. That is not to suggest that radiometric dating is grossly inaccurate to the point that the planet Earth could be just a few thousand years old, but merely that constant temperature and pressure are never a guarantee, particularly over periods of time that span more than one human lifetime, because there is not one particular constant individual who could possibly have made an observation to verify that situation. (The prior criticism of radiometric dating is NOT suggesting that the Earth is only thousands of years old.) Many of those who are suspicious of the idea that an all-powerful God created the universe are unable to reconcile the idea that the Earth appears to be billions (or perhaps only millions) of years old, with the Biblical account of the origin of man, which would suggest that mankind has only been in existence for approximately 6, 000 years. Atheists and agnostics anxious to mock those who might suggest that dinosaurs were aboard Noah's Ark to escape the Great Flood will be disappointed to know that there is a possible alternate explanation besides a young Earth. The book of Genesis describes Satan as *the serpent*. Although some respected scholars of God's Word [34] hold the position that the book of Genesis makes no reference to a Pre-

Adamic race, still it clearly would not be a stretch to conclude that the fallen angels that followed Lucifer (the serpent and the Counterfeit Light) were reptiles (dinosaurs) as well, and that their physical bodies had perished. Scriptures in a couple of places in the Old Testament suggest that perhaps there was a time gap between the events that God performed that is referred to in Genesis 1:1 and 1:2 of God's Holy Word.[32] In the Holy Bible, the Book of Psalms in the 102nd psalm, verse 25 says, "Of old you laid the foundations of the earth, and the heavens are the work of your hands."[35] Also God's Word perhaps provides another clue, as the book of Jeremiah in the fourth chapter of the prophet's book possibly could be implying that God indeed destroyed the Earth to the point that it was void and full of darkness before He breathed the first breath into Adam.[36]

Curiously enough, scientists from Vanderbilt University, Columbia University, and the University of Ohio have reached the conclusion that between 100 and 200 million years ago, a meteor near 1000 feet in diameter weighing in excess of 100 million tons and traveling more than ten miles per second, struck the planet earth in the northwest middle region of Tennessee with a shattering impact, thus forming a crater four miles in diameter and one-half mile in depth that is now known as the Wells Creek Basin. **"Shock waves raced in all directions, and a fiery mushroom cloud of fine rock dust and debris rose high in the air"**[37] according to the historic marker on Highway 149 in front of the Highland Rim Head Start office and **Mike Baldwin of the Memphis Archaeological and Geological Society.** [38]

As it probably took months for the dust to settle,

plant and animal life (dinosaurs perhaps) that managed to

survive the disaster may have perished due to a lack of

sunlight, and an extreme variance in temperatures.

(Photo on the previous and next page is of both sides of a sign near the Houston and

Stewart County line that describes the catastrophic event in the Wells Creek basin of northwest

middle Tennessee.)

THE WELLS CREEK BASIN

Scientists believed the earth's surface appeared to be damaged forever. Millions of years passed and erosion and vegetation softened this ugly scar left by the impact. The rim of shattered rock disappeared, and the level of adjoining land was lowered hundreds of feet by erosion. Since its discovery, geologists have studied this phenomenon. It was discovered about 1860 when railroad construction revealed rock formations that suggested a violent event had occurred. This marker is located close to the center of the impact.

A much larger meteor struck the Earth near the Yucatan Peninsula [39] approximately 65 million years ago that created a 150 (about 100 miles) kilometers wide crater. It is believed to have been an event that may have caused the extinction of the dinosaurs. Events like these might certainly be interpreted to be confirmation of scripture referring to God's wrath being poured out on the Earth from Heaven [40], as He destroyed the cities of fallen angels who had defied Him and followed Lucifer. This would have occurred before God created Adam. [41]

Bibliography

1)Wallace, J.Warner, Cold Case Christianity

http://coldcasechristianity.com/2015/why-the-origin-of-the-universe-is-important-to-the-case-for-gods-existence-video/

(2)Slater, Sara, Where did the matter in the Universe Come from?/ Ask an Astronomer/ Cornell.edu

http://curious.astro.cornell.edu/about-us/101-the-universe/cosmology-and-the-big-bang/general-questions/570-where-did-the-matter-in-the-universe-come-from-intermediate

(3)Ellman, Roger, The Problem of Big Bang Matter vs. AntiMatter Symmetry (abstract), arxiv.org

https://arxiv.org/ftp/physics/papers/0007/0007058.pdf

(4)Sutton, Christine, Antimatter: Physics, Encyclopaedia Britannica

http://www.britannica.com/science/antimatter

(5)Nova Evolution, Scientist Michio Kaku Surprised with finding Irrefutable Evidence: God Does Exist, NovaEvolutionOficial.blogspot.com,

http://novaevolutionoficial.blogspot.com/2015/05/scientist-michio-kaku-surprised-with.html

(6)Matthew J. Parry-Hill, Robert T. Sutter, and Michael W. Davidson - National High Magnetic Field Laboratory, **Basic Electromagnetic Wave Properties**, FSU.edu,

http://micro.magnet.fsu.edu/primer/java/wavebasics/

(7)The Holy Bible, King James Version, Romans 1: 24-32, Bible.com,

https://www.bible.com/bible/1/rom.1.24-32.kjv#

(8)The Holy Bible, New International Version, **Deuteronomy 22:5**, BibleGateway.com,

https://www.biblegateway.com/passage/?search=Deuteronomy+22:5

(9)The Holy Bible, New King James Version, **John 1:9, Biblia.com,**

https://biblia.com/books/nkjv/Jn1.9

(10)The Holy Bible, New King James Version, **John 1:10, Biblia.com**,

https://biblia.com/books/nkjv/Jn1.10

(11)The Holy Bible, New King James Version, **John 1:1, Biblia.com**,

https://biblia.com/books/nkjv/Jn1.1

(12)The Holy Bible, New King James Version, Revelation 21: 22-25, Biblia.com,

https://biblia.com/books/nkjv/Re21.22

(13)Ibid, Revelation 21: 22-25, Biblia.com,

https://biblia.com/books/nkjv/Re21.22

(14)The Holy Bible, First John 1:5, Biblia.com,

https://biblia.com/books/nkjv/1Jn1.5

(15) Matthew 27, Grace to You,

http://www.gty.org/resources/bible-qna/BQ032913/why-did-jesus-cry-my-god-my-god-why-have-you-forsaken-me

(16) Significance of veil/ Got Questions,

http://www.gotquestions.org/temple-veil-torn.html

(17)The Holy Bible, New King James Version, Revelation 21: 22-25, Biblia.com,

https://biblia.com/books/nkjv/Re21.22

(18) Lucifer/ Behind the Name,

http://www.behindthename.com/name/lucifer

(19)The Holy Bible, Isaiah 14: 13 and 14, New King James Version,

https://www.biblegateway.com/passage/?search=Isaiah+14%3A13-14&version=NKJV

(20)The Holy Bible, Isaiah 14: 12, New International Version, BibleHub.com,

http://biblehub.com/isaiah/14-12.htm

(21) The Holy Bible, Genesis 1: 2, King James Version, BibleGateway.com

https://www.biblegateway.com/passage/?search=Genesis+1&version=KJV

(22)Frankenberry, Nancy K., The Faith of Scientists: In Their Own Words, Princeton, NJ: Princeton University Press 2008, pgs 145-147

(23) The Left's Playbook: Satanist Saul Alinsky's 13 Rules for Political Warfare/ DC Clothesline,

http://www.dcclothesline.com/2014/09/10/lefts-playbook-satanist-saul-alinskys-13-rules-political-warfare/

(24)Shamoun, Sam, Allah as a Deceiver: Examining Satan's Accusations Against the Integrity of Allah

http://www.answering-islam.org/Shamoun/allah_deceiver.htm

(25)The Holy Bible, New International Version, Isaiah 40:8, Biblegateway.com

https://www.biblegateway.com/passage/?search=Isaiah+40:8

(26) Constitution of the Commonwealth of Massachusetts, Article III

https://malegislature.gov/Laws/Constitution

(27) Erick Erickson/ Red State

http://www.redstate.com/erick/2015/09/23/karl-rove-got-planned-parenthood-its-komen-money-back-wants-you-to-fund-it-too/

(28) Einstein, Albert, Ideas and Opinions, New York: Three Rivers Press (Crown Publishers 1954 and 1982), pg 46-47

(29) The Holy Bible, New Kings James Version, Romans 14: 10-11, Biblia.com,

https://biblia.com/books/nkjv/Ro14.10-11

(30) The Holy Bible, New King James Version, 2nd Chronicles 7:14, Biblia.com

https://biblia.com/books/nkjv/2Ch7.14

(31) The Holy Bible, New King James Version, Esther Chapters 7-10,

https://biblia.com/books/nkjv/Es7

(32) The Age of the Earth/ USGS.gov,

http://geomaps.wr.usgs.gov/parks/gtime/ageofearth.html

(33)Stewart, Don, What Was the Covenant God Made with Noah?, BlueLetterBible.org,

https://www.blueletterbible.org/faq/don_stewart/don_stewart_745.cfm

(34) Stewart, David J., The Bible Teaches an Old Earth, but a Young Human Race,

http://www.jesus-is-savior.com/Evolution%20Hoax/old_earth-young_man.htm

(35)The Holy Bible, New King James Version, Psalms 102: 25,

https://biblia.com/books/esv/Ps102.25

(36) The Holy Bible, New King James Version, Jeremiah 4:23-28,

https://biblia.com/books/esv/Je4.21

(37) Tennessee History for Kids, Houston County, TnHistoryForKids.org,

http://www.tnhistoryforkids.org/local/houston

(38)Baldwin, Mike, Wells Creek Impact Crater: Stewart and Houston Counties, Central Tennessee, Rockhound News, http://www.memphisgeology.org/images/rocknews0306.pdf

(39)Evolution, What Killed the Dinosaurs?, Public Broadcasting System,

http://www.pbs.org/wgbh/evolution/extinction/dinosaurs/asteroid.ht ml

(40)The Holy Bible, Jeremiah 4: 23-28, BibleHub.com,

http://biblehub.com/commentaries/jeremiah/4-23.htm

(41) Stewart, David J., Fallen Angels Prove Old Earth, Jesus-Is-Saviour.com,

http://www.jesus-is-savior.com/Evolution%20Hoax/fallen_angels.htm

Chapter 2

Man's Place in God's Universe

Man's Place in God's Universe

For those who have already arrived at the only correct answer to the question of causation (God created *everything*, in case you are a little slow.), there is a deeper question. *What is our (the human race) place in a universe created by The Great I Am, the Original Light?*

Adam and Eve were created for the Lord's pleasure, as with all living things that He created, so that He could have fellowship with them.[42] As a collective group we as members of the Family of God have a destiny that He has carefully planned out. Part of that destiny involves sharing His Light that has changed our lives with others. The old negro spiritual[43] and often sang children's Bible school song, [44]*This Little Light of Mine* reminds Christians that they are not to be "secret agent"[45] Christians and hide the Light of Jesus under a *bushel* that is shining and glowing brightly around them from the overflowing joy that has their hearts filled to the brim. As Jerry Baysinger at C-faith, Freedom in the Word wrote, *"There are many Christians who are blending in so well with the world, that it's impossible to tell them from the lost and unsaved. They say they bear the name of Christ, but that's where the similarity ends."*

Some of these "secret agent" Christians often spend their Sunday mornings in church, looking at their watches, yearning for the clock to move along so that they can get home just in time for kick-off. This breed of Christian that lives in the Mountain or Pacific time zone frequently checks the internet on his or her telephone to catch the first or second quarter scores, because some of the games sometimes begin at 10 a.m. or 11 a.m. Their

prayers may even be schizophrenic or borderline

blasphemous, *"Praise you Lord for everything. Please help*

me grow closer to You Lord.......And oh yeh, could you help

the Broncos pull through this week?" Other Christians

also allow activities outside the church to start to crowd

in on their time with the Lord[46], and henceforth get in

the way of the primary objective that Our Savior gave us,

which is to share His Light with others and to make our

primary focus to be fishers of men.

Rather, Jesus told believers to "go and make

disciples of all nations, baptizing them in the name of the

Father, Son, and Holy Spirit."[47]

One of the amazing qualities of the Lord that many

people experience when having an encounter with

Yahweh or Jesus is the brilliance of His glory. Recently, a young lady of a prominent Muslim family came to know Jesus, *The Original Light* when a presence came into her room at Midnight[48] and lit up her room up as though the sun were shining through the window. A voice spoke to her telling her that she was a sinner, and she knew it was Jesus. The encounter almost mirrors the experience that Saul of Tarsus had with Our Lord and Savior on the road to Damascus.[49]   Saul was an enthusiastic slayer of the followers of The Lamb of God, and his encounter with Jesus, the Original Light was the beginning of a transformation that molded him into one of the leaders of the early church and into Paul, the apostle who is believed to have written more New Testament books than any other follower of The Way.[50]

Indeed, the Son of righteousness, allows for the forgiveness of all sin for those who repent. He is the Original Light whom is also the *Sun* of righteousness[51] as Charles Wesley posthumously reminds believers every year when they sing the Christmas hymnal *Hark the Herald Angels Sing*. He (Jesus) allows for those who will follow Him to be healed, and to tread down the wicked as ashes under the soles of their feet.[52] The Lamb of God, the Original Light died for all, but eventually gives up to uncleanness [53]those who reject His gift of salvation in favor of their own sinful desires and choose to repeatedly oppress those who love Him and serve Him. He is the *Sun* of righteousness, because no artificial light that was made by Him or by those that He created is worthy of worship. We know that those who worship the sun are in error because the prophet Isaiah in verses 19 and 20 of

Chapter 60 of The Word tells us:

"[19] The sun shall be no more thy light by day;

neither for brightness shall the moon give

light unto thee: but the LORD shall be unto thee an

everlasting light, and the days

of thy God thy Glory.

[20] Thy sun shall no more go down; neither shall thy

moon withdraw itself: for

the LORD shall be thine everlasting light, and the

days of thy mourning shall

be ended."[54]

The Great I Am is the Everlasting Light, the *Original Light,*

Who created man in His image. He created man so much

in His own image, that gradually over hundreds of years,

man has been able to unravel some of Jehovah's secrets.

 However, just as a limit of a function in the mathematical

discipline of calculus sometimes approaches infinity

without ever reaching a destination, such is man's success

in unraveling the complexity of God's secrets.[55] God is

light, travels at the speed of light or faster, has brilliance

radiate from His very being. Man can take matter that

has been created by God, cause it to burn after decreasing

its energy of activation, and achieve at least a momentary

release of energy that includes some form of

electromagnetic radiation.[56] He can imitate God's infinite

ability to generate energy merely from His glory and

presence. Men of science and technology can do amazing

things with light energy, as evidenced by the invention of

photoelectric cells and lasers (that emit tertiary light), nuclear power and fiber optics, space travel, and semi-conductors, all of which can be traced back to Albert Einstein's theories on relativity and quantum mechanics.[57]

Men with brilliant minds comparable to Einstein can generate and manipulate matter and energy but only for a *finite* amount of time. It takes these men sometimes an entire lifetime to accomplish what The Great I Am (The Original Light) dashes into reality with a mere whisper or touch of His hand.

Though God radiates light, and *is* light, that does not mean that all light is God, as even man can create the circumstances in which both visible light and other energy is released [58], and sometimes makes intellectual leaps to explain mysteries of the Original Light. Albert

Einstein imagined himself riding alongside a beam of light through space. He hypothesized that gravity bends light. Einstein's hypothesis has now been bolstered by what scientists at the Jet Propulsion Laboratory at the California Institute of Technology have observed to have occurred in space, as NASA's Kepler space telescope helped physicists and astronomers observe the effects of a dead star bending the light of its companion star.[59] Einstein had also hypothesized that the physical phenomenon known as gravity was a warping of space and time. He came up with equations that describe how the curvature of light (or other matter) resulted in a distortion of the four dimensional fabric of space and time.[60]

He (The Great I Am) is the Original Light that reveals, energizes, and vitalizes us,[61] and is capable of doing so with no other resources, because HE is the source of all sources[62]. We do not carry our own light. We carry God's Light. As we grow closer to Him, His presence begins to grow within us. That growing presence within each of us begins to radiate the glory of the *Original Light*.[63] We are able to have an impact on others not because of our superior intellect, nor because of our tenacious willpower, but because of the power of God's Light that is within us.[64] In his letter to the people of the church in Ephesus, the Apostle Paul wrote:

[8]For you were once darkness, but now *you are* light in the Lord. Walk as children of light[65].

Walking lockstep in righteousness with the Light is indeed a joyful experience as we grow in His extended grace and mercy. Our will becomes closer and closer to what the Holy Spirit wills in our daily lives. The prompting of the Holy Spirit ultimately causes the righteous to rejoice and the flame in the lamp of those who choose wickedness in lieu of His gentle urges to be snuffed out.[66] Anyone who continues to draw closer to God gradually starts to desire His righteousness in lieu of past desires. The believer is now able to be made righteous by God's gift of redemption through the death of Jesus, who paid the ultimate price for all of his or her sins, and not through any works of his or her own.[67] Anyone who has experienced the joy and peace of the Holy Spirit, and has elected to move away from the Original Light will never be able to take as much pleasure in sin as they used to, as his or her knowledge of the truth makes for absolute misery in the midst of darkness. The "fullness of the backslider's misery will come out of his own ways, and the fullness of the good man's content will spring out of the love of God which is shed abroad in his or her own heart."[68]

The joy and peace of Jesus, which makes the innermost depths of the heart and soul feel content should not be mistaken for an absence of trials and hardship in everyday life. Though that inner joy and peace felt within breeds a calm, serene confidence, it should not be presumed that everyday life all of a sudden is "a breeze" because the "magic Jesus" is there for all who believe. Trials and tribulations are within the lives of believers, perhaps even more so than those of non-believers. That noticeable visible outer glow oftentimes noticeably radiating from a recently born again Christian comes from Jesus, the Original Light[69], and is an indication of a newfound strength that allows believers to endure what may have previously been considered to be unbearable or unachievable. That same powerful inner strength helped the Apostle Paul and most of the disciples of Jesus maintain their joy even though they were repeatedly beaten and even killed [70] for preaching the Gospel of Jesus. Similarly, "many Christian activists have lost their liberty during the last 80 years, as they have endured persecution because of their faith in Christ, and have leaned on the Holy Spirit to maintain hope through perilous times for believers. For example, some Chinese House Church leaders were imprisoned for 20 to 30 years. They served their term and went straight back to preaching the gospel,"[71] even though they understood that doing such a thing may involve more persecution, imprisonment, or that it could even cost them their lives.

Pastor Saeed Abedini [72] spent more than eight years in Evin prison in Teheran, Iran. He was repeatedly tortured and persecuted for his belief in Christ. In a letter to his wife, the pastor wrote:

"This is another golden opportunity for me to shine the light of Christ in this dark world and to let God use me. [73]

The prayers of many Christians for Pastor Saeed resulted in America's leaders, including President Barack Obama, intervening on his behalf. However, **the pastor has still endured persecution from Satan** [74] even after being freed from prison and returning to the United States. Whether guilty or innocent of conduct that he is accused of, it is clear that he is involved in a spiritual battle. He is a target of Satan because of his stand for Jesus. Prayers for

Pastor Abedini to be able to be still and let the Lord go before him can allow for restoration of what the locust has eaten[75], and for the resolution of his dire situation to be used for furthering the Kingdom that is at hand. We are all sinners and have fallen short of the glory of God[76]. As we die daily to Christ[77], He is able to cleanse all of the areas in which each of us fails miserably. We are able to openly admit our failures, claim the blood of Jesus for forgiveness. As we grow closer to the Holy Spirit, our desire to repeat those same shortcomings fades, and through Christ, we are strengthened[78]. Pastor Saeed Abedini's trials within the United States have the same potential to let Christ's light shine as his captivity in Iran did. His association with other men of God like Franklin Graham shows that he is interested in letting that very thing happen.

Others[79] who have been used in a great way by God have fallen short, but sought the Lord and came clean about their deception[80]. Though many outside the Christian body have been quick to criticize impropriety, the willingness of Christians in the spotlight to repent of their sin frees God up to extend His mercy and even use them in a bigger way[81].

The joy and peace of Christ also gives those whom are the targets of secular persecution the courage to stand up against unjust civil ordinances. Towns all across the nation are attempting to force Christian businesses to provide services to same sex couples even though God's Holy Word strictly forbids sexual relations between people of the same gender. Breanna Koski and Joanna Duka, owners of Brush & Nib Studio based in Phoenix,

Arizona, a business that seeks to honor God through their art. They specialize in hand painting, hand lettering, and calligraphy for events, like weddings. The Alliance Defending Freedom filed a motion of preliminary injunction in Arizona Superior Court for Brush & Nib. The complaint stated that if If Koski and Duke were to turn down creating art to celebrate a same-sex marriage, the city of Phoenix could fine them up to $2,500 for each day they violate the law and make them spend six months in jail, since their studio creates art for opposite-sex wedding ceremonies. Jonathan Scruggs, legal counsel for Alliance Defending Freedom[82], said in a statement[83].

"Government can't censor artists or demand that they create art that violates their deepest convictions."

Indeed, the persecution of believers in Christ actually affords the opportunity to let the Light of Christ shine as they decline to yield to those with political power who bow down to the artificial light, the Prince of Darkness, Lucifer. As the believer shows the courage to stand against error and for Divine Truth, and "is willing to bear ridicule, slander, loss and persecution of all kinds"[84], he or she reflects the Light of Jesus just as the moon reflects the sunlight in our solar system. How one worships God during trials and tribulation is much more of a reflection of how close to the light one has become than how one basks in God's glory during the abundant and less turbulent times, as the Lord even allowed Satan to deprive Job of all that he had in the world [85]. He lost his family and almost all of his worldly possessions, yet remained faithful to the Lord. Eventually God restored what Job had to even more than he had previously. He had proven to the prince of darkness that Job was faithful to Him (Jehovah) despite all the trials and tribulations that were piled upon him.

In order for someone to find where he or she fits in perfectly in God's universe, there is a need for a certain awareness for where he or she is with relation to our Lord. Plants are able to quickly maximize their growth potential by sending auxins[86] (a class of hormones) to the underside of leaves to aid cytokinins in the promotion of the synthesis of DNA[87]. The resulting build-up of cells on the underside of the leaf results in the largest possible amount of surface area on the upper side of the leaf being faced toward the light, resulting in more energy being available for the process of photosynthesis to fuel the activities of the plant, including more growth. Moving toward the light allows a particular plant the opportunity to maximize its potential to produce more energy, to stimulate growth, and thus allow for even more movement toward the energy providing light source.

Similarly, modeling and looking towards the Original Light[88] (Christ) will aid one in having a clear purpose, maintaining a clear direction, and excellent focus on Him, so that a reflection of Him [89] will be clear for others to see as well.

(Photograph on the next page depicts Zach Noble participating in the CrossWalk near Dover, TN. He was unaware at that moment that light was shining down on the cross that he was carrying.)

Photograph taken by Danny Peppers, owner and publisher of the Stewart County Standard, 316 Donelson Pkwy, PO Box 543, Dover, TN 37058

As one (or any of us) moves toward The Original Light, the Great I Am, a zeal to be in His presence begins to grow. Noah and Abraham both knew what it was like to walk with God, as did Enoch. He (Enoch) became so close in his walk with God that He was taken into the presence of God's radiant glory without experiencing death. Although being so clear of worldly desire is an obstacle in growing closer to the light of Yahweh, He has given us Yeshua (Jesus) to wash away our sin and the Holy Spirit so that we might "experience the Light of the glory of God that is to be found in Him".[90] In the 27th Psalm David wrote,(verse 1) "The Lord is my light and my salvation". Being in His presence and glory is more than our sinful bodies are able to bear, but as we walk with Christ and we allow Him to clean up our lives through the revelations of the Holy Spirit, (verse 14) waiting on the Lord strengthens our hearts.[91] The more purified our hearts become, the more our bodies are able to withstand the radiance and power of God's glory. Though we seek God's face, almost every member of the human race with the exception of Enoch and Elijah have yet to experience this extreme cleansing of the heart and soul. Moses, God's trusted servant was protected by His hand and a crevice in a rock, so that the extreme power of the glory of The Original Light would not harm him.[92] Sadly, rather than growing and walking in step with God, most of us have experiences that are more similar to those of Martin Luther than those of the prophet Elijah, who grew so close to God that eventually he rode off into heaven in a flaming chariot. [93] Our insistence on leaning on our own understanding and giving in to the desires of the flesh allow for brief encounters in which we approach God's vicinity and holiness, but our unwillingness to walk lockstep in unison with His desires causes us to be more distant from Him than we would like, because God can not tolerate sin. Our reluctance to stop yielding to the flesh is just enough of a barrier to keep us from approaching the face of Yahweh until we allow Jesus to finish the work of cleaning that He is continually doing in our lives.

Although Luther's conclusion that man could only be saved through faith and grace alone, and not by works[94], was indeed inspired by the Holy Spirit, His outspoken criticism of the Catholic Church regarding the selling of indugences most certainly was a principle that was instilled in him by the Holy Spirit as well. However, such deeds as advocation of the expulsion of Jews from the German empire and the condoning of the practice of polygamy leave questions in the minds of followers of Jesus as to how close Luther was to the Almighty at the time of his death. The Jewish people are God's chosen people according to His Word[95]. In the book of Deuteronomy, the seventh chapter and the sixth verse God's Holy Word tells us,

"You are a people holy to the Lord your God. The Lord your God has chosen you out of all the peoples on the face of the earth to be his people, his treasured possession".[96]

Although many Jews, as well as many Gentiles will perish if they do not accept God's gift of redemption that was given to mankind through the descendents of Abraham via the lineage of King David of Judah, God still honors the covenant between he and Jacob (Israel). He gave them a new way to enter His presence, as it is impossible for any man to live up to God's Law. The blood of animals is no longer required as a sacrifice for sin. The blood of Jesus, the Lamb of God serves as the eternal sacrifice for whomever will repent of his or her iniquities and follow the path of The Original Light. Those who follow The Original Light will be eternal inhabitants of the New Jerusalem, a much more glorious place than the Jerusalem built by God's chosen people in the Promised Land[97]. Included in those whom may be followers of The Original Light, whom is also known as The Word, are the descendents of Ishmael and Esau. If they acknowledge that Jesus is Lord, they often endure much persecution, and are often even martyrs for Christ, such as the Ethiopian lady Workitu[98], whose willingness to die at the hands of her Islamic husband rather than renounce her faith in Jesus, resulted in the conversion of her two sons and at least one of her Muslim friends to the acceptance of Christ[99]as their Lord and Saviour. In addition, several of ther town's leaders took note of her courage in death and have expressed a desire to know more about Yeshua. The attempt by Workitu's Islamic husband and and thuggish Muslim friends to intimidate her into hiding the Light of Christ that was shining within her backfired. Her death has served to magnify HIs glory and perhaps even to eventually lead most of her village to embrace the love and mercy of the Son of God, who died for them as well, so that God the Father might count them as righteous through the sacrifice of HIs blood. Jesus promised all of us, that if **we lose our lives for His sake, then we will gain life in Him.**[100] For most of us, the actual losing of life is not literal or physical, but losing ownership of ourselves to Christ. We must yield to Him in every way in order that He can begin to work within us. We must do this with our life as a whole, and die to Him daily as well, denying our old carnal natures on a continual basis in submission to the Original Light, Who now lives within us[101] and has a path laid out for us that is quite different from one that we might choose for ourselves. Our old self must learn to yield to the will of the Holy Spirit.

Bibliography

(42)King James Bible Online/ Revelation 4: 11,

https://www.kingjamesbibleonline.org/Revelation-4-9_4-11/

(43)This LIttle Light of Mine/ NegroSpirituals.com,

http://www.negrospirituals.com/songs/this_little_light_of_mine.htm

(44)Veggie Tales- This Little Light of MIne/ Metrolyrics.com

http://www.metrolyrics.com/this-little-light-of-mine-veggie-tales-ml-video-wmt.html

(45)Baysinger, Jerry, Secret Agent Man/ C Faith- Freedom in the Word,

http://www.cfaith.com/index.php/blog/27-articles/your-destiny/16988-secret-agent-man

(46) Sports vs. Church, Family Discipleship Path,

https://familydiscipleshippath.com/2013/11/22/sports-vs-church/

(47) The Holy Bible, King James Version, Matthew 28: 19/ BibleHub.com,

http://biblehub.com/kjv/matthew/28-19.htm

(48) Hohmann, Leo, **Muslim Ruler's Daughter Arrested for Christian Faith**/ WND.com,

http://www.wnd.com/2016/04/muslim-rulers-daughter-arrested-for-christian-faith/

(49) The Holy Bible, New King James Version, Acts 9: 1-7, BibleGateway.com,

https://www.biblegateway.com/passage/?search=Acts+9&version=NKJV

(50) Sect of "The Way", "The Nazarenes" & "Christians" : Names given to the Early Church, **Bible Things in Bible Ways**, biblethingsinbibleways.wordpress.com,

https://biblethingsinbibleways.wordpress.com/2013/11/21/sect-of-the-way-the-nazarenes-christians-names-given-to-the-early-church/

(51) Richardson, William E., Charles Wesley/ **Lights4God.wordpress.com**,

https://lights4god.wordpress.com/2012/12/18/charles-wesley/

(52) The Holy Bible, New King James Version, **Malachi 4: 2**, Biblia.com,

https://biblia.com/books/nkjv/Mal4.2

(53) The Holy Bible, New International Version, **Romans 1:24-25**, BibleStudyTools.com,

http://www.biblestudytools.com/romans/passage/?q=romans+1:24-32

(54) The Holy Bible, King James Version, **Isaiah 60: 19-20**,

https://biblia.com/books/kjv1900/Is60.19-20

(55) **Infinite Limits**, Paul's Online, Lamar University,

http://tutorial.math.lamar.edu/Classes/CalcI/InfiniteLimits.aspx

(56) **Kinetics: Activation Energy**, Chemistry Department, Texas A&M,

https://www.chem.tamu.edu/class/majors/tutorialnotefiles/activation.htm

(57)Isaacson, Walter, <u>Einstein: His Life and Universe</u>, (New York: Simon & Schuster 2007), pg 5

(58)Groleau, Rick, **The Science of Fire**, NOVA, PBS.org,

http://www.pbs.org/wgbh/nova/physics/science-fire.html

(59)Klavin, Whitney, **Gravity-Bending Find Leads to Kepler Meeting Einstein**, NASA.gov,
http://www.jpl.nasa.gov/news/news.php?release=2013-124

(60) Isaacson, Op. Cit, pgs 3 and 4

(61)Stedman, Ray C., God is Light/ RayStedman.org,

http://www.raystedman.org/new-testament/1-john/god-is-light

(62)The Holy Bible, New International Version, 1 Corinthians 8:6, BibleHub.com,

http://biblehub.com/1_corinthians/8-6.htm

(63)Jackson, John P., The Unstoppable Power of God's Light, StreamsMinistries.com,

http://www.streamsministries.com/resources/spiritual-gifts/the-unstoppable-power-of-god-s-light

(64)Jackson, John P., Ibid., , StreamsMinistries.com

http://www.streamsministries.com/resources/spiritual-gifts/the-unstoppable-power-of-god-s-light

(65)The Holy Bible, New King James Version, Ephesians 5:8,

https://www.biblegateway.com/passage/?search=Ephesians+5%3A8&version=NKJV

(66)The Holy Bible, New King James Version, Proverbs 13:9, BibleStudyTools.com,

http://www.biblestudytools.com/nkjv/proverbs/13-9.html

(67)Taylor, Justin, *What Does Paul Mean by the Righteousness of God?*, TheGospelCoalition.org,

https://blogs.thegospelcoalition.org/justintaylor/2010/10/13/righteous
ness-of-god%E2%80%9D/

(68)Spurgeon, C.H., **How a Man's Conduct Comes to Him**, *A sermon (No. 1235) delivered on Lord's Day Morning, May 16th, 1875, at Metropolitan Tabernacle, Newington,* BibleBB.com,

http://www.biblebb.com/files/spurgeon/1235.htm

(69)The Holy Bible, New International Version, **Hebrews 1:3**, BibleGateway.com,

https://www.biblegateway.com/passage/?search=Hebrews+1

(70)Curtis, Ken, **Whatever Happened to the Twelve Apostles?**, Christianity.com,

http://www.christianity.com/church/church-history/timeline/1-300/whatever-
happened-to-the-twelve-apostles-11629558.html

(71) **2 Corinthians6v3to13**: PAUL'S HARDSHIPS, jrtalks.com,

http://www.jrtalks.com/2Corinth/2cor6v3to13.html

(72) BeHeardProject.com/Saeed,

http://www.BeHeardProject.com/Saeed

(73)SaveSaeed.org: Saeed's Letter/ You Tube,

https://www.youtube.com/watch?v=NvTS-V0nxc0

(74)Beaty, Katelyn, The CT Interview: Saeed Abedini Answers Abuse Allegations, ChristianityToday.com,

http://www.christianitytoday.com/ct/2016/may/ct-interview-saeed-abedini-abuse-allegations-prison.html

(75)The Holy Bible, Joel 2:25, English Standard Version, BibleHub.com,

http://biblehub.com/joel/2-25.htm

(76)The Holy Bible, Romans 3: 23, King James Version, KingJamesBibleOnline.com,

https://www.kingjamesbibleonline.org/Romans-3-23/

(77) The Holy Bible, 1 Corinthians 15: 31, The Complete Jewish Bible, BibleStudyTools.com,

http://www.biblestudytools.com/1-corinthians/15-31-compare.html

(78)The Holy Bible, Phillipians 4: 13, New King James Version, BibleGateway.com,

https://www.biblegateway.com/passage/?search=Philippians+4%3A13&version=NKJV

(79)A brief History of Day Star, DayStar.com,

http://www.daystar.com/about/

(80) Daystar Founder's Affair: "Caught Up in Success"/ CBN News,

http://www.cbn.com/cbnnews/us/2010/december/daystar-network-founder-admits-extramarital-affair-/?mobile=false

(81)About Marcus Lamb, MarcusLamb.org,

http://www.marcuslamb.org/about-marcus-lamb/

(82)Jessen, Leah, Phoenix Artists Threatened with Jail Time if They Don't Serve Gay Weddings, DailySignal.com,

http://dailysignal.com/2016/05/16/phoenix-artists-threatened-with-jail-time-if-they-dont-serve-gay-weddings/

(83)Scruggs, Jonathan, Jail Time for Phoenix Artists Who Disagree with Government?, Alliance Defending Freedom, ADF.org,

http://www.adfmedia.org/News/PRDetail/9939

(84) Lenski, R.C.H, Commentary on the New Testament: Matthew, Peabody, MA: Hendrickson, 2001, p. 203 via Jackson, Jason, Let Your Light Shine, Christian Courier,

https://www.christiancourier.com/articles/1229-let-your-light-shine

(85) The Holy Bible, Job 1:12, King James 2000 Bible, BibleHub.com,

http://biblehub.com/job/1-12.htm

(86)VIB (the Flanders Institute for Biotechnology). (2012, April 16). **Why plants grow towards the light**, *ScienceDaily*. Retrieved May 27, 2016 from www.sciencedaily.com/releases/2012/04/120416101028.htm

(87) Skoog, F. and Miller, C.O. (1957) Chemical regulation of growth and organ formation in plant tissue cultured in vitro. Symp Soc Exp Biol XI: 118–131 via **Kantharaj, G.R.**, Plant Hormones-**Cytokinins**, GRKraj.org,

http://plantcellbiology.masters.grkraj.org/html/Plant_Growth_And_Development5-Plant_Hormones-Cytokinins.htm

(88)Macphearson, Jay, **The Church: Growing Towards Christ**, SermonCentral.com,

http://www.sermoncentral.com/sermons/the-church-growing-towards-christ-jay-mcphearson-sermon-on-unity-120211.asp

(89) The Holy Bible, **2 Corinthians 3:18**, God's Word Translation, BibleHub.com,

http://biblehub.com/2_corinthians/3-18.htm

(90)Sorge, Bob, **The Secret of Walking with God**, Christian Bible Studies: Transformed by the Truth, ChristianityToday.com,

http://www.christianitytoday.com/biblestudies/articles/theology/secret-of-walking-with-god.html

(91) The Holy Bible, **Psalms 27**, Biblia.com,

https://biblia.com/books/kjv1900/Ps27

(92) The Holy Bible, Exodus 33: 22, Douay-Rheims Bible, BibleHub.com,

http://biblehub.com/exodus/33-22.htm

(93) **What is the background story of Elijah the Prophet?**, GetSmarter.com,

http://get.smarter.com/qa/world-view/background-story-elijah-prophet-ee1e8acbb11de6a4?ad=semD&an=gemini_s&am=broad&o=34532

(94)Martin Luther and the 95 Theses, **The Significance of Martin Luther's Work**, History.com,

http://www.history.com/topics/martin-luther-and-the-95-theses

(95)Got Questions?org, What does it mean that the Jews are God's chosen people, GotQuestions.org,

http://www.gotquestions.org/Gods-chosen-people.html

(96)The Holy Bible, Deuteronomy 7:6, English Standard Version, Biblia.com,

http://biblia.com/bible/esv/Deut%207.6

(97)The Holy Bible, **Leviticus 26:42**, New International Version, BibleHub.com,

http://biblehub.com/leviticus/26-42.htm

(98)Bieszad, Andrew, **Muslim Husband Beats His Wife to Death for Becoming a Christian, Now Both Her Sons AND Their Muslim Friends Have All Become Christians**, Shoebat.com,

http://shoebat.com/2016/04/30/muslim-husband-beats-his-wife-to-death-for-becoming-a-christian-now-both-her-sons-and-their-muslim-friends-have-all-become-christians/

(99)Smith, Samuel, **Muslim Brothers Turn to Christ after Watching Slain Mother Beaten for Converting to Christianity**,ChristianPost.com,
http://www.christianpost.com/news/muslim-brothers-turn-christ-watching-slain-mother-beaten-converting-christianity-162597/

(100) The Holy Bible, **Matthew 16: 25**, Berean Study Bible, BibleHub.com,

http://biblehub.com/matthew/16-25.htm

(101) DePra, David A., **Why Christians Suffer**, GoodNewsArticles.com,

http://www.goodnewsarticles.com/suffering.htm

Image Credit: Trail Missions

Pictured above: Trail Missions team member Lela Roby (partially visible) shares how the blood of Jesus cleanses our hearts from sin with her new Zambian friends.

Chapter 3

A God of Miracles

Yahweh is indeed a God of miracles.   He performs

miracles of healing that cannot be explained by modern

medicine. **He reveals His miraculous power as He**

chooses as He shows His strength among the nations.[102]

The Church of the Resurrection in Jerusalem claims that the Miracle of Holy Fire takes place every year on the first Sunday after the spring equinox and Jewish Passover.[103]

The Church of the Resurrection in Jerusalem claims that the Miracle of Holy Fire takes place every year on the first Sunday after the spring equinox and Jewish Passover.[103] Sometimes God Chooses to make His presence obvious through showing His Light or "Holy Fire". The photograph of young Garrett Noble carrying the cross included on page 33 of this book is an example of that. God chose to let believers in the miracle of the Resurrection of Jesus see a glimpse of His Light. On October 10, 2015, the day that the photograph was taken by Danny Peppers, owner and publisher of the Stewart

County Standard in Dover, Tennessee, more than twenty people participated in a Cross Walk. They started at the Sanctuary Church in Dover and travelled about ten miles to nearby Papa Rock. The beam of sunlight that can clearly be seen shining down on the cross carried by Garrett Noble was not apparent until the photograph had already been taken.[104]

Perhaps greater than the miracles that appear to deceive the eyes though, are the changes in people's lives[105] that take place through the burn of the Holy Fire. A famous song by Christian artist Jeremy Camp named *Empty Me*[106] prays for the Holy Spirit to help him make these changes with the lyrics,

"Holy fire, burn away, my desire for anything.............
that is not of you, but is of me.............

because I want more of you, and less of me....

Empty me, empty me.............

Won't you fill me?"

The interesting point that this song makes is that a gradual purification through His Holy Fire indeed is how God molds and shapes us. The Holy Spirit inspires us to do things that are holy and pleasing to God. That same Holy Fire makes us know in our heart and soul when a particular thought, action, or attitude is not reflective of the light of Christ as well. Fire always produces change. It forces us to act or respond. **Fire often brings focus into our lives through trials**[107], which force us to recognize flaws within our lives. As we walk with the Holy Spirit through trials that we experience in our daily lives, old desires, habits, and attitudes are burned away. These parts of our character are often replaced with gifts from the Holy Spirit that we as new creatures in Christ can embrace. We are transformed into new creatures as the Holy Spirit gives us each separate portions of the nine spiritual gifts as He sees fit. We are then driven to strive for Word of knowledge, Word of wisdom, the ability to prophesy, the possession of enduring faith, the ability to channel God's healing power, the power to channel God's miracles, the knack for spiritual discernment, the talent for speaking various languages (tongues), or the gift of language (tongue) interpretation.[108] Our time spent utilizing gifts from the Holy Spirit[109] with a pure heart that is truly dedicated to glorifying the Great I Am results in the very transformation of our being. We truly become vessels that can be filled with the Light of the Holy Spirit so that we overflow with His radiant glory. We also become mirror images of the Original Light so that those who are around us in our daily lives start to experience walking with Him vicariously. They start to want what we have. They aren't quite sure what *it* is, but they can see that whatever the cause, *it* has transformed us for the better. Their curiosity is at a peak level and they are ripe for the harvest. They have become ready to jump into the saving net of Jesus. We have become fishers of men because we have allowed the Holy Spirit to have His way in molding and shaping us, burning away those character flaws that are unpleasing to Him. In order to be used of God according to His perfect plan and will, "all the junk, all the imperfections, all of the sins, all of self must be removed" from our lives.[110]

God, the *Original Light* is a God of righteousness. He has power over sin and the original being that defied Him and inspired rebellion against light and nourished an affinity for evil darkness. Jesus, the Word has authority over demons[111], the fallen angels whom were cast down with the *counterfeit* light, Lucifer. He routinely casts demons out with a single command, although He set the example and actually prayed and fasted in order to exorcise a demon.[112] Likewise, we should follow His example and engage in prayer and fasting as a necessary preparation for spiritual warfare. Unfortunately, non-believers are generally at the mercy of evil spirits as many modern psychologists try to explain away demonic possession[113] by attributing the diabolical behavior to mental disorders that are then routinely "treated" with psychotrophic medications that the first psychiatrists to design these types of drugs referred to as "chemical lobotomies[114].

Trail Missions team members Renae Black Roby and Lela Roby pray for a woman who was tormented

by evil spirits and complained of a racing heart in Zambia, Africa.

Photo by Jack Mututwa

Trailmissions.net

https://www.facebook.com/jmututwa/posts/10153679467057896

Indeed, the Great I Am is the Original Light. He (Yahweh, Jesus, The Great I Am, The Original Light) also said, "Let there be light!" Just the utterance of His Word brought the energy charged photons into existence. Because He is all-powerful, The Original Light is also a God of healing. It should come as little surprise that, not only is visible light beneficial to mankind, but that the electromagnetic radiation that lies outside the spectrum detectable by the human eye can be beneficial to the human body as well. According to **MedPage Today**, *"electromagnetic radiation in the near-infrared -- wavelengths just beyond the approximately 700-nm limit to human vision -- can affect cell and organism* *biology*"[115]. One of the effects that has been observed in multiple tissue types is an increase in ATP production inside individual cells. God is the Original Light. He created electromagnetic radiation and visible light. He said, "It is good," and indeed in doses of moderation varying wavelengths of the electromagnetic spectrum have properties that stimulate healing and nurturing to the human body. Low level exposure to ultraviolet radiation aids the human body in the production of Vitamin D, which is a facilitator in the absorption of calcium and phosphorus, elements that are critical in the processes of bone development.[116] **The Massachusetts Institute of Technology now reports**[117] that the capability exists to even view soft as well, that the capability exists to even view soft as well as hard tissue using X rays, meaning that the need for the presence of a contrasting agent would be lessened or even no longer existent in order to view the human body under the layers of protective skin.

The healing power of the Original Light, the Great I Am is unlimited for He is the source of *all* energy. The countless miracles performed throughout the Holy Bible by Jehovah, the Father, Son, and Holy Spirit are reminders to us that He is The Great I Am and is not bound by any physical laws of this universe. He created those laws and can change them on a whim. Men like Albert Einstein, J. Robert Oppenheimer, Enrico Fermi, Crawford Greenwalt, Percival Keith, Vannevar Bush, James B. Conant, Ernest O. Lawrence, Edward Teller, Eugene Wigner, Jon von Neumann, Leo Szilard, and women like Lisa Meitner helped humankind unleash the secret of the immense power that is located inside just one atom of uranium[118]. That power was used to bring World War II to an end as the Japanese cities of Hiroshima and Nagasaki virtually were blown off the map and Japan lost its will to fight. That power demonstrated on August 6 and August 9, 1945[119] is a mere fraction of the power, glory, and magnificence of the Great I Am. The unleashing of the energy held within atoms of uranium produced an awesome display of power that devastated two cities and killed thousands of people, and yet the most powerful way to unleash God's power does not lie within the realm of science, but within the willingness to forgive our fellow man. God only forgives us so much as we are willing to forgive others who have hurt us deeply. The surest way to move toward the Original Light in the manner that Enoch and Elijah did is to show the same grace and mercy to others that God Himself does[120]. Loving our brothers, and our enemies as well, doing good for them at every turn, is the path that **assures us of being children of The Most High**[121], who can move toward the Original Light for an eternal and joyous fellowship.

That's a memory that I know I won't forget," said Tate Roby via Facebook of the man in the photo above. Tate added, "When he was asked if he wanted a ride he immediately said yes. He then crawled to his hut and changed clothes and we got him in his chair. It was a priceless moment!"

Bibliography

(102) The Holy Bible, Psalm 77: 14, God's Word Translation,

BibleHub.com, http://biblehub.com/psalms/77-14.htm

(103) Holy Fire, Description of the Miracle of Holy Light (Holy Fire) that Happens Every Year in Jerusalem, HolyFire.org, http://www.holyfire.org/eng

(104) The Stewart County Standard, Tuesday October 13, 2015, Volume 1, Issue 21, page 1 photo caption

(105) Roby, Shayn, We Love You Gary, and Holy Fire Rests in our Hearts and Souls, Shaynroby.wordpress.com, https://shaynroby.wordpress.com/2013/02/10/we-love-you-gary-and-holy-fire-rests-in-our-hearts-and-souls/

(106) Camp, Jeremy, Empty Me, Video Uploaded to You Tube by EMI Music, YouTube.com, https://www.youtube.com/watch?v=TWk42LFOQXM

(107) Tentmaker, Fire in the Bible, Tentmaker.org,

http://www.tentmaker.org/BreakingBread/1.html

(108) The Holy Bible, 1 Corinthians 12: 7-11, English Standard Version, Biblia.com,

https://biblia.com/books/esv/1Co12.1

(109) Nine Gifts of the Holy Spirit, Bible-Knowledge.com,

http://www.bible-knowledge.com/gifts-of-the-holy-spirit/

(110) Todd, Susan E., Are You the Potter or the Clay?, 1Timothy4-13.com,

http://www.timothy4-13.com/files/proverbs/potter.html

(111) The Holy Bible, Mark 1: 21-27, New King James Version, Biblia.com

https://biblia.com/books/nkjv/Mk1.21

(112) The Holy Bible, Matthew 17: 21, Aramaic Bible in Plain English, BibleHub.com, http://biblehub.com/matthew/17-21.htm

(113) Brown, Tom, How to Cast Out Demons, Tom Brown Ministries, TBM.org

http://www.tbm.org/castoutdemons.htm

(114) Brainwashed by Psychotropics, DrAxe.com,

http://draxe.com/brainwashed-by-psychotropic-drugs/

(115) Gever, John, Infrared Light Therapy Runs Ahead of Science, MedPageToday.com,
http://medpagetoday.com/Neurology/GeneralNeurology/43985

(116) Health Effects of Ultraviolet Radiation, Government of Canada, HealthyCanadians.gc.ca,
http://healthycanadians.gc.ca/healthy-living-vie-saine/environment-environnement/sun-soleil/effects-uv-effets-eng.php?_ga=1.53159648.996177826.1484071525

(117) Chandler, David L., A Leap Forward in X-Ray Technology, MIT News,

http://news.mit.edu/2013/a-leap-forward-in-x-ray-technology-1203

(118) Who Built the Atomic Bomb?, Atomic Heritage Foundation,

http://atomicheritage.org/history/who-built-atomic-bomb

(119) Bombing of Hiroshima and Nagasaki, History.com,

http://history.com/topics/world-war-ii/bombing-of-hiroshima-and-nagasaki

(120) Forgiveness, Act 17: 11 Bible Studies, Acts 17-11.com,

http://www.acts17-11.com/forgive.html

(121) The Holy Bible, Luke 6: 27-37, New King James Version, BibleStudyTools.com,
http://www.biblestudytools.com/nkjv/luke/passage/?q=luke+6:27-37

Image Credit: Tate Roby, Facebook

Believers from Stewart and Houston Counties in Middle Tennessee en route to participate in working witness and evangelism for Trail Missions Ministries in Zambia, Africa. Pictured above are, Left to right: Warner Roby, Cass Rye, David Mitchell, Lela Roby, Scott Roby, Renae Roby, and Tate Roby.

A Personal Word from the Author

Why did I decide to write this book? I accepted Jesus as my Lord and Savior in 1978 at age 11 when I was in the 6th grade, and I was very sincere when I did so. As the years went by, I tried to be a Burger King Christian. I attempted to get away with doing it my way whenever I could. Of course, I probably didn't fool very many people. I certainly didn't fool the Lord, but I managed to do a great job of deceiving myself. I fit the profile of the Secret Agent Christian that was mentioned earlier in this book.

While touring through Satan's diversionary path, I found myself addicted to multiple ways of falling short of His (the Original Light, The Great I Am) glory. Although during the years of serving myself instead of Jesus I did manage to get a Bachelor of Science degree from Bethel College (now University) in McKenzie, TN, and got Tennessee and California teaching credentials in biology through Trevecca Nazarene University in Nashville, TN, I still was trying to do things my way and knew that I was falling fast into places that I had no business being. My wakeup call came while I was teaching biology and coaching football in Southern California. Out of respect for well known friends who have passed on, and for keeping the old life in the past, the dirty details will presently remain unspoken. Some of these details may be revealed when the Lord leads me to believe that the time is right to help others, but for now the specifics will remain in that city commonly known as Las VAGUE-us (Forgive the horrible pun!!).

People who were obedient to Christ in California played a huge role in bringing me, a 48 year old prodigal son, home to my parents in Stewart and Houston counties in Tennessee, who have served as ministers and missionaries in the Church of the Nazarene, the United Methodist Church, and through numerous independent ministries. Currently, my parents are serving the Lord in Zambia Africa with Jack and Amber Mututwa. If it were not for Jack and Amber's work in Zambia, my wife Heather and I would not have met. We were married on May 18, 2015, after only meeting a couple of months before. It was the culmination of a couple of years of obedience and prayer, as I specifically asked God for Heather before I really knew her, and the Lord actually sent her home from church at **Long Creek Church of the Nazarene near Dover, Tennessee** [122] with me in a tiny pickup truck with my father and I. We are open to serving on the mission field. We are both in agreement and are in constant mindful prayer that God, the Original Light, will indeed shine on a path that is unmistakably clear that we are to follow. I have previously served as an interpreter on mission trips throughout Mexico, as I am fairly fluent in Spanish, but am open to wherever God sends Heather and I.

In 2007, I found myself trapped in sin in so many different ways and checked myself into **The House of Jeremiah** [123] , (which was sponsored by **Calvary Chapel of Downey, CA,** [124] but is now a part of the ministry of Prison Ministry of America) of my own free will. Although I can not report to anyone that I completed the entire program there (I *bolted* twice.), I can honestly say that I kept allowing the Holy Spirit to mold me as I had to die to

Christ daily. Hopefully, dying to Him Daily at least most of the time involved falling short in a different manner than the previous day's offense. That hasn't always been the case, but when it wasn't, the Holy Spirit dealt with me even more strongly, and spanked me a little bit for my defiance. The good Christian folks in Orange County, California helped feed me spiritually. Pastor Keith Andrews of **Wayside Christian Fellowship in Orange (now in Anaheim),**[125] and Pastor Wiley Drake of the **First Southern Baptist Church in Buena Park, CA** [126] both extended their open arms to me in kindness and Christian love, most of the time when I didn't even ask for their help. They provided spiritual guidance and even helped guide me away from a relationship that was harmful to me as I couldn't quite close that door myself, even though

I didn't want to be defiant to what God was trying to tell me.

In 2010, I began writing right wing political commentary at **The Conservative Underground** [127] and slowly but surely began to learn how to navigate through several blogging platforms. In 2012, I was writing an article about how America was at a crossroads and happened across an article that was similar to mine that had been written by James Robison at Glenn Beck's website, *The Blaze*. I almost instantly knew that I was supposed to attend the *Under God Indivisible* [128] event and made plans to attend the events that took place on Friday, July 27, 2012. As the day approached, I became aware that other events organized by Glenn Beck and FreedomWorks were taking place as well, including

Restoring Freedom at the Mavericks Arena, and Restoring Love at Cowboys Stadium. Listening to so many God anointed speakers and mingling with so many people of a like mind during that week lit a fire in me that has continued to this day. It inspired me to start blogging at **Roby's Right Corner** [129] (a Blogger site), at **The Original Light** [130] and **ShaynRoby** [131] (both Wordpress sites).

Publishing numerous articles at my blog sites eventually led to a little bit of national recognition, as Joe Messina at The Real Side has been kind enough to occasionally repost a few of my articles, the first of which was written about the Snapchat Selfie Killing in Jeannette, Pennsylvania, and was titled at The Real Side, "**Shayn Roby: Kids Need Jesus**". [132]

The Holy Spirit, over the course of several years, has guided me in writing this book. Although I have worked as a science teacher, substitute teacher, manual laborer, and as a direct support professional in the mental health field, which took up most of my time, I nevertheless kept the vow to attempt to write down at least one complete thought and at least one documented reference source per day, and it has resulted in the first book that the Lord has led me to publish, *The Original Light*.

Bibliography

(122) Long Creek Church of the Nazarene, Dover, TN

http://app.nazarene.org/FindAChurch/details.jsp?q=creek&id=1118
78

(123)The House of Jeremiah

http://www.ccdowney.com/ministries/ministry-list/house-of-
jeremiah/

(124)Calvary Chapel, Downey, CA

http://www.ccdowney.com/

(125) Wayside Christian Fellowship, Anaheim, CA

http://waysidefellowship.com/

(126 First Southern Baptist Church of Buena Park, CA,

Facebook page,
https://www.facebook.com/fsbcobp/?hc_ref=PAGES_TIMELINE

(127) The Conservative Underground Blog,

http://www.tcunation.com/

(128) Under God Indivisible Conference

Arlington, TX: July 27, 2012

http://www.lifetoday.org/undergodindivisible/

(129) Roby's Right Corner

http://www.shaynroby.blogspot.com/

(130) The Original Light

http://www.TheOriginalLight.wordpress.com/

(131) Shayn Roby

https://www.shaynroby.wordpress.com/

(132) Roby, Shayn, **Shayn Roby: Kids Need Jesus**, The Real Side,

http://www.TheRealSide.com/2015/02/shayn-roby-kids-need-Jesus/

Image Credits

Danny Peppers

Owner and Publisher

Stewart County Standard

dpeppers@StewartCountyStandard.com

news@StewartCountyStandard.com

ads@StewartCountyStandard.com

931-232-3801

316 Donelson Pkwy.

PO Box 543

Dover, TN 37058

Jack Mututwa

Trail Missions/ Zambia, Africa

American Contact:

Trail Missions

PO Box 13205

Scottsdale, AZ 85267

Jeremiah 29: 11:

"For I know the thoughts that I think toward you, says the Lord, thoughts of peace and not of evil, to give you a future and a hope."

Made in the USA
Charleston, SC
20 February 2017